:
_____

om:
_____

/   /
date given

/   /
date redeemed

MW00903130

YOU

FINE DINING

Reserve a table for two
at a fancy restaurant and we'll linger over
appetizers, entrées, and desserts.

WEEKEND
GETAWAY

: _____

om: _____

/ /
date given

/ /
date redeemed

YOU·OWE·ME

WEEKEND GETAWAY

Take me on a glorious weekend
away from it all.

:

om:

/ /

date given

/ /

date redeemed

YOU·OWE·ME

SURPRISE ME

Let's do something
we've never done before.

:
_____

om:
_____

/ /
date given

/ /
date redeemed

YOU·OWE·ME

HAPPY UNBIRTHDAY
TO ME!

Give me a present for
no reason at all.

A MASSAGE

To:

From:

/ /
date given

/ /
date redeemed

YOU·OWE·ME

A MASSAGE

One hour, no less.
If you're not up to it, feel free to hire a pro.

:

om:

/   /

date given

/   /

date redeemed

YOU·OWE·ME

DINNER IN

Home-cooked or delivered—
it doesn't matter as long
as we eat by candlelight.

THE GREAT
OUTDOORS

_____ :

_____ om:

/   /

date given

/   /

date redeemed

YOU•OWE•ME

THE GREAT
OUTDOORS

Let's make our
escape to nature.

BREAKFAST
IN BED

e:
_____

om:
_____

/   /
date given

/   /
date redeemed

YOU·OWE·ME

BREAKFAST IN BED

Please don't forget
the newspaper.

COUPON POTATO

e:

_____

om:

_____

/   /

date given

/   /

date redeemed

YOU·OWE·ME

COUCH POTATO

Turn off the phone—
it's all about you, me, a pile of DVDs,
and buttered popcorn.

PARTY!

:_____

om:_____

/ /
date given

/ /
date redeemed

YOU·OWE·ME

PARTY!

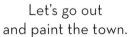

Let's go out
and paint the town.

YOU·OWE·ME

A LOVE LETTER

Because sometimes it's nice
to see it in writing.

YOU·OWE·ME

DINNER AND
A MOVIE

You pick the place,
I pick the flick.

EXPAND MY
HORIZONS

: _____

om: _____

/ /
date given

/ /
date redeemed

YOU·OWE·ME

EXPAND MY HORIZONS

Share your creative side
with me and take me to an art show,
a reading, or a concert.

LET'S HOLD
HANDS

: _____

om: _____

/ / _____
date given

/ / _____
date redeemed

YOU•OWE•ME

LET'S HOLD HANDS

And go on a nice, long walk,
with no particular destination.

PUBLIC
DISPLAY OF
AFFECTION

: _____

om: _____

/ /
date given

/ /
date redeemed

YOU • OWE • ME

PUBLIC DISPLAY
OF AFFECTION

Show other people
how much you love me.

YOU·OWE·ME

FINE DINING

Reserve a table for two
at a fancy restaurant and we'll linger over
appetizers, entrées, and desserts.

e: _____

om: _____

/ /
date given

/ /
date redeemed

YOU·OWE·ME

WEEKEND GETAWAY

Take me on a glorious weekend
away from it all.

SURPRISE
ME

:

om:

/ /
date given

/ /
date redeemed

YOU·OWE·ME

SURPRISE ME

Let's do something
we've never done before.

HAPPY UNBIRTHDAY TO ME!

to: _____

from: _____

___ / ___ / ___
date given

___ / ___ / ___
date redeemed

YOU·OWE·ME

HAPPY UNBIRTHDAY
TO ME!

Give me a present for
no reason at all.

EXPAND MY
HORIZONS

_____ :

_____ om:

/ / /
date given

/ / /
date redeemed

YOU•OWE•ME

EXPAND MY HORIZONS

Share your creative side
with me and take me to an art show,
a reading, or a concert.

LET'S HOLD
HANDS

: _____

om: _____

/ /
date given

/ /
date redeemed

YOU·OWE·ME

LET'S HOLD HANDS

And go on a nice, long walk,
with no particular destination.

:
_____

om:
_____

/ / /
date given

/ / /
date redeemed

YOU·OWE·ME

PUBLIC DISPLAY
OF AFFECTION

Show other people
how much you love me.